MW01031117

World Stage Press

Verse from the Village

confessions of a
Firework

1.   My life must look a lot like the fourth of July.

upon arrival, I light the sky bright, loud, and
temporary.
I am a beautiful explosion, but only for a moment.
a pyrotechnic poet; a short lived spectacle.
I have always wished I were more fireplace
than firework.

                              -From ADHD: a list of fears and confessions

4

confessions of a

Firework

Poems & Prompts by
Angela Aguirre

World Stage Press
Verse from the Village

World Stage Press
Verse from the Village

Copyright © 2016 by World Stage Press

ISBN-13: 978-0-9858659-8-6

ISBN-10: 0-9858659-8-9

All rights reserved. No part of this publication may be
reproduced, distributed, or transmitted in any form or by any
means, including photocopying, recording, or other electronic
or mechanical methods, without the prior written permission
of the publisher, except in the case of brief quotations
embodied in critical reviews and certain other noncommercial
uses permitted by copyright law.

Printed in the United States of America

Layout Design by Nadia Hunter Bey
Cover Design by   Undeniable Ink
Copy Editing by Marilyn Forrest

For my Pintoresca Poets.

The incredibly talented students, on the cusp of adulthood I have had the honor to teach. YOU are the spark I needed to light the fire that became this book. You gave me a reason to stop talking about it and start being about it. And that was more powerful than any of the irrational fears I could've conjured up.

You are my why.

In loving memory of my Daddy
Ernesto "Crazy Ernie" Aguirre

1947-2011

CONTENTS

Identity

Love

Heartbreak

Death

Growth

Womanhood

FORWARD

I remember the first day I met Angela. She was the kind of girl who understood beauty but couldn't exactly identify it in herself. She had on the "right" clothes. She was stylish. Her face was painted as if a photo shoot was happening, but there she was in the dimly lit dinning room of an estate in Los Feliz taking my workshop about Re: Connecting with the artist in you-Vulnerability and Integrity. I start every class by congratulating them. My class is tough, is it not for those who want to remain shallow or in hiding, it will bust you completely out of your comfortable little life into the one you have always secretly wanted. I don't remember much else about those first interactions with her. What I do recall is over the following year or so becoming clear that I was not interested in a closer friendship than casual acquaintances. We had a mutual friend circle so our lack of closeness was becoming more and more apparent. I would hear rumors that Angie was upset with me about this or that and I would brush it off. I am several years older than Angie, at the time I was the only female host and producer of Da Poetry Lounge (the nations largest weekly poetry venue) and found that my role was even more important than I realized. I became aware of how careful I had to be in developing relationships with people that supported the venue and equally careful because frankly for some people I was a vehicle into the "inner circle."

I recall a night when Angie called me and asked why we weren't friends. I think I asked her if she wanted the truth, she said yes, and I told her: I don't have reckless friends, I don't want to worry about you all the time and if we are friends then I will have to. I don't want to get a phone call about you killing yourself in a car accident or whatever." She was silent for a moment and said something to the effect of "no one has ever said this to me before."

11

In the years since then, Angie has become a friend and sister. Her family has become my family, her heartbreak and joy my own. It is thrilling to watch her become. I feel like a mama bird of sorts because I remember that first day, her nervous energy, her telling me she had no intention of reading a poem out loud but look at her now, all wings and halo. I share with you these stories to give context to what a privilege reading this collection will be, because Angie had to become herself to have access to it. She had to give up a bunch of her bullshit, pride, ego, hurt feelings and just write. She had to stay committed not only to the idea but to the finished product. This is her coming of age story, her rite of passage, this book is her paying it forward. I celebrate those brave enough to grow in a world that will entice you to stay small and childish. So read this book when you are hurting, when you are filled with love, share these poems with the love of your life or a person you simply know is not but wish could be. It took every day of Angie's life to have all these experiences to share them with you.

Angie, I could not be more proud. Bless you and all that you touch. Your heart is pure, your temper is fading and your love, well your love is always in full bloom.

Natalie Patterson
Poet & Teaching Artist
Los Angeles, June2015

PREFACE

"Everybody is a genius. But if you judge a fish by its ability to climb a tree, it will live its whole life believing that it is stupid." -Albert Einstein

I believe we are all good at something. And when I say "good" I don't mean "good" as in average. I don't mean "good" as in replaceable. I don't even mean "good" in the way we mean it when some random person on the street asks us how we are, and we respond on auto-pilot by answering "good." I believe we are all here to do something. One single thing that only *you* can do the way *you* can do it. With that said, I believe I was born to be a poet and a teacher. With my career, I have chosen to be in a position of influence. I have chosen to devote my energy to organizing young people and inspiring them to create things that shape the world. I have chosen to spend my time convincing them they are worthy. But before you congratulate me on this, you must first know how ironic it is. Truth be told, fear and inadequacy have been the prevailing themes in my own life. I have allowed fear to stop my arms from reaching. I have let it convince me that mediocrity was my birthright, and that all of the strange stirrings I'd feel when in the presence of greatness; were not calling me, but taunting me. After being clinically diagnosed with depression, anxiety, and ADHD in 2008, I began therapy and the long journey toward healing from the irrational scars these disabilities had left behind. I began to realize that they had managed to slither their way into almost every aspect of my life. But it wasn't until I began teaching that I really began to hold myself accountable.

It is emotionally exhausting to look my students in their eyes week after week and sincerely tell them to follow their dreams while running from my own. It was my students who helped me see how tired I really was. Tired of idle dreams, and unrealized ideas. Tired of being aware of my potential. Tired of

13

being tormented by that relentless voice inside me that begs me to create, but ignoring it in fear of the world's reaction to the outcome. My mind has always been an idea factory. They come to me as easily and often as oxygen. Ideas for organizations, creative collaborations, marketing campaigns, poems, movies, ways to make things work more efficiently, better ways to teach lessons, and an endless list of other ideas that have been abandoned along the way.

As an artist, poet, teacher, woman and human being I have had to face the fact that ideas; in and of themselves mean nothing. Ideas without follow-through are just dreams. And dreams, well dreams... don't pay the rent. Dreams don't get you a degree. They don't finish paintings or films or create things that make the world a better place. Dreams don't finish books and they damn sure don't show the world what you are capable of.

This book is my first public attempt at bravery. It is my attempt at bringing one of these dreams out of my head and into my hands. This book is an act of practicing what I preach. In the process of creating it, I have embraced what I am good at. I have stopped allowing my irrational thoughts to paralyze me, and I have broken the cycle of fear. I hope this book finds you wherever you are in your journey, and offers you a place to rest.
I want you to know that you are not alone.

Love,
Angie

confessions of a
FIREWORK

Identity.

"I can't seem
to stay out
of my own way."

— Gloria Anzaldua

ADHD: a list of fears and confessions

1. I fear that my legacy will be an unfinished
    poem. like the ones that fill my notebook;
    I do not want to look back and see that I could've
been so much more than I turned out to be.
2. My life is a series of almost's.
I fear that I will never know greatness. that I will not be
able to stay around long enough to even become good
enough to be great, at anything.
3. I often feel like I do not belong.
Like a concert in a library, a red dress at a funeral
I am a magnet for wide-eyed looks.
I have learned that people will not always
tell you when your defect is showing, But their eyes will.
brows raised in confusion; it is more polite
to say you are 'one of a kind' than to try understanding
why. They will say you are 'unique.'
Claim variety is the spice of life, laugh it off, and dismiss
the moment because it feels too much like a turtle neck
in the Summertime. These compliments will always feel
more like insults.
4.   I am in a perpetual state of barely getting by. of
     trying to catch up. ironic that someone so 'full-
     speed ahead' can so easily get left behind.
5. When people tell me I am amazing
I do not believe them. I smile, give thanks and hope not
to be discovered. I am a fraud.
If only they knew that my accomplishments
feel a lot more like accidents.
As if the universe sometimes makes mistakes
in my favor. Like a glitch in the solar system;
a data error.

Someone, somewhere,
must have spelled my name wrong.
I hope no one notices.

6.   The best of intentions with the worst execution. I am what happens when a brilliant idea meets a terrible mistake.

7.   My life must look a lot like the fourth of July.
upon arrival, I light the sky bright, loud, and temporary.
I am a beautiful explosion, but only for a moment.
a pyrotechnic poet; a short lived spectacle.
I have always wished I were more fireplace
than firework.

8.   I have a love-hate relationship with a pill bottle.
I am now at 60 Mg of Adderall a day.
When I don't take it, I feel useless.
When I do, the dry mouth plagues me and I am less myself, but maybe that is a good thing. People say they see the difference. Say I am more pleasant and agreeable. Sometimes I wonder if I am medicated to make everyone else's life easier.

9.   I wish my life were easier.
wish I wasn't such a problem.
such a series of unfortunate events.
There are only so many apologies you get,
until "I'm sorry" is no longer enough.

"To live in the Borderlands means you
are neither *hispana india negra española
ni gabacha, eres mestiza, mulata,*
half-breed
caught in the crossfire between camps
while carrying all five races on your back
not knowing which side to turn to,
run from;

To live in the Borderlands means knowing
that the *india* in you, betrayed for 500
years,
is no longer speaking to you,
that *mexicanas* call you *rajetas,*
that denying the Anglo inside you
is as bad as having denied
the Indian or Black...

Cuando vives in la frontera
people walk through you,
the wind steals your voice"

-Gloria Anzaldua

Borderland

Mi querida Gloria tells me
I am a borderland.
A hybrid. A creature of the middle.
Yo Soy una frontera.
I am a borderland.
my identity is a crossroads.
She wants me to celebrate this.
a meeting place of two worlds.
I was born into a cultural limbo
between my mother's blue eyes
and my father's brown hands.
Ni de aqui, Ni de alla
I am a bridge. A road. I belong in between.
but Gloria, If I am Not from here
and I am Not from there
then where will I celebrate?
Notice the indigenous in my cheekbones.
Watch my olive skin sing songs of a country
I know nothing of.
Look at my hair.
watch it mimic black silk falling flat
against my back It reminds me to stand straight
to dawn my last name like the badge of honor
that it is. But still, I am not enough.
this hair this skin this name this blood
is not enough to give me a home
cannot make home of somewhere
I have never lived.
Yo soy una frontera.
You can hear it in my Spanish
can see it in my eyes

each time I scan the room
before I roll my r's
It is in the shame of knowing I can pass
as a white girl if I need to.
ni de aqui, ni de alla
"It must be so easy for you" She said.
"to be able to choose.."
As if I ever had a choice.
I am a borderland.
always on the outside looking in.
everything about me longing for a home.

Recovery

I was born into recovery.
dim rooms that smelled of
cheap coffee and the serenity prayer
chairs in a circle and surrender in the air;
I was raised at a meeting.
amidst rock bottom stories and second chance dreams.
I was born into Narcotics Anonymous.
a path toward hope for the helpless
12 steps closer to the beautiful aftermath of chaos.
I was born into restoration.
into finding the courage to change.
and taking moments of silence
for the addict who still suffers.
I was born into fellowship;
newcomer chips and sober livings
taking inventory and understanding
that life only happens "one day at a time"
I was born into Sunday barbecues;
to the sounds of Motown music and East LA barrio
slang. growing up, birthday parties were always
sober events with guest lists that sounded more like
a cell block roll call; I grew up sharing toys with the sons
and daughters of ex-convicts with hearts that bled for us
and smiles that hid behind thick mustaches and lip liner;
L o v i n g parents with too many tattoos
and mile long rap sheets;
I learned early on not to judge anyone
by what they used to be;
my childhood taught me to look past the past
to see the perfect in progress

and that l i v i n g the part will always be more
important than l o o k i n g it.

Depression

When your bones shape shift
into barbwire and your hands
hide behind your back, willingly.
When your conscience
becomes a warden-
and you start to move
as if your feet are shackled together-
You know it is back.
That seductive lullaby
Ready to cradle you, infant
and rock you back into submission.
It is time.
To prepare yourself
to go back underground.
Back into the cold, damp
depths of your prison.
not the one of this world-
but the one you create in your madness.
The one you, yourself,
own and operate
like a one woman freak show.
Behind the barred windows of your eyelids
This prison is as real as any.
Depression;
is so much more than just being sad.
It is the bleeding of the spirit.
A battle that is not concerned
with the size of your army,
or the power of your weapons,
And in spite of all your best efforts
You just can't seem to win.

26

Anxiety

When it comes
I split in two.
one of me,
still sane
embarrassed at the antics
of my other half;
trying to reason with her.
the other,
a tea kettle
foaming at the mouth;
her bones
quickly outgrowing
the lifeless weight of her body.
time is her enemy.
never has been on her side.
and then,
just like that;
the battle is lost.
they merge.
the insanity
devours any logic
that may be left in the room
and there I am
the worst version of myself
deranged
wanting to crawl out of my own skin
and even more reckless than the girl
who wakes up without her head.
everyone knows she can't be trusted.
I am never certain of what the outcome will be.
I cry and clench my fists

to keep the demons at bay.
they live inside me
like the empty house that I am.

I just want to go home.
but when it comes
I have no idea where that is.
or even where I want it to be.
everything fits 10 sizes too small.
it is scary
to feel ashamed of being what you are.
especially
in front of the only person
who has wanted to know you from the inside out.
pathetic
to let the walls cave in
when he is looking;
we are only supposed to do this in private.
in public
we must flex our sanity.
treat it like peacock feathers;
something to attract the opposite sex.
but he knows now
that my smile lied.
that my arms
never could
s t r e t c h
wide enough
to hold it all together
and I am not sure
they ever will.

The Cost Of Joy
For Robin Williams

The sad clown
always leaves the party too early.
"We paid him for two hours"
They'll say.
"He only stayed for one...
He can forget a tip."
Selfish.
They have no idea the cost of joy
for the saddest of clowns.
The energy. The magic tricks.
The Balloon animals.
The ease with which
he danced around the room.
From costume changes
to voice impressions.
As if genius can be quantified
in a dollar amount.
The highs are so high.
But the lows,
Unfathomable.
When your smile lights up the world-
it is not okay to frown.
It is not okay to take off the costume.
To be a real person
with real problems
To be a disappointment
to your fans.
Meeting you,
is always supposed to be an
'Experience'

Clowns are not
supposed to be sad.

Oh, but we are.
Living this way Is always heavy.
It is always too much to carry.
Your arms are always tired
And your shoulders,
They always ache.
Your body always feels like it has
known too many tragedies.
But some days you feel strong.
Strong enough
to dead lift that mountain you carry.
Strong enough to hold it up
with one arm, show it off,
and revel in your self-control.
There are even years you claim superhero,
Convinced you have mastered
the art of hiding your landscape.
Temporarily
turning your peaks into valleys
foolishly thinking
You have bulldozed the problem-
But you always seem to forget-
how the water levels rise in Summer.
When winter comes,
the waters return to Ice
and your mountain is revealed.
The cold wind
begins to swirl around your head
Until it reaches your toes,
Sending chills back up to the tips of your fingers -
And you remember who you are.

The Summer always
has a way of making us forget.
Suddenly,
Your clothes start to drown you.
You are a child again.
Helpless. Hopeless.
Filling your own shoes
Becomes physically impossible.
Your voice begins
to sound borrowed.
Depression
is a slow and
painful death.
A silent killer.
It is the unfillable hole.
The unquenchable thirst.
A desperate longing
for something
Something
it seems
that does not exist.

Identity: In Borderlands, I turned my cultural identity into a metaphor. If you could turn any aspect of your identity into a metaphor what would it be? Start a line with "I am a _____" and use the following stanzas to explain why this is true.

*Hint: My mother is Italian and my father was Mexican. I use the word "borderland" to explain what it feels like to be in the middle of two cultures.

_____

_____

_____

_____

_____

_____

_____

_____

_____

_____

_____

_____

_____

_____

_____

Love.

Love

Loving someone does not mean you understand them
it means you are willing to.
willing to remain uncomfortable in the process
willing to say you are sorry
when you have no idea what you've done.
it means you are willing to stay
even when your anger is telling you to leave
even when the little boy in you tempts you
with the possibility of greener pastures;
loving someone is a choice.
after the lust fades and the honeymoon is over
love is what is left when it is no longer about the chase.
Love is what is left when it is no longer convenient
when her makeup is smeared
and his feet smell
and their attitudes are blocks of salt
love, is morning breath and sacrifice.
laundry and burnt steak. Fighting and make up sex.
working together and sharing secrets
believing in each other and telling it like it is
love is unrefined. it is raw and untrained.
it has no idea what it is doing most days
but it shows up anyway.
Love is creating new problems
and facing them together.
it can shape shift you into the person
you were always meant to be.
Love has the power to change us
but only
if we are willing to be changed.

Brito

The first time I heard his name
it was in the octave of divine.
not because it is somehow more than just a name,
but because I had never heard you
make this sound before.
The syllables were melodic, like you had to muster up
all of the jazz inside your body
just to say you knew him.
you sang him transcendent.
the way women sing of men
when they are no longer concerned
with mundane things, like time and distance.
Like I had never seen you smile before.
as if your whole life you have been pretending to make
half-moon of your mouth; when all this time you were
really just trying to the show the world how sharp your
teeth are.
you have been living in the prison of your
mother's shadow since you met her.
you have no business loving in shadows
the way she did; you were born with a wildfire inside
your chest. you were made to lantern the world with it.
you are a daughter of the sun,
a creature of luminescence.
Your silhouette is made of light
don it and walk forward toward the place that
exists between
black and white;
the place that houses the intangible laughter
you swore yourself
too monochrome to remember.

welcome. this, is where it will happen.
you will recall the excruciating joy
that comes from loving someone on purpose;
it is a feeling so irrationally beautiful
you will not be sure you are as committed
to sanity as you once thought yourself to be
here, you will be given back all of the things you
thought you lost.
it will be here, in the place where your words become
saccharine things;
that you will meet yourself for the very first time
over and over again.
This is the gray area where truth lies; in naked silence.
there is nothing more pure
than the wide eyed optimism
the fresh air of the beginning brings
breathe it in deep now.
rest here, as long as you can. emerge.
undress yourself and reveal the whole of you.
lie raw with him in the moments
you cannot bring yourself to do anything
but love him in;
love him,
until he gives you a reason not to.

Maybe

Maybe I cut my chest open way too often.
Maybe my friends are right.
Always spilling my insides
into these poems,
ready and willing.
Hoping I've found the real thing.
Hoping I've found someone
worth all of the ink inside my pen.
I want to write something
worth memorizing
about someone worth keeping.
So maybe they are right.
they say I love like Skydiving,
that I let myself fall on purpose.
They say this is dangerous.
That I do everything too fast.
But what other choice do I have?
I have never been anyone else.
Only ever been this girl
with arms outstretched,
and a body that is loyal
only to the one that it craves.

I was born in fastforward.

So it is hard to think of another way to live,
let alone another way to love.

I am not sure I want one.
I hope I never meet a man
who makes me want to stop trying.

I would rather risk a broken heart
than be the owner of one that doesn't work.

I would rather write honest poems
about conjured up voodoo
and Long Island listeners,
Than lie about being content without
the possibility of heartbreak.

To love is human.
and I crave it.
the way I have always craved the skin,
smell, kiss, and touch of each man I have loved thus far

Love is as human
as any mistake
I have ever made.

What is wrong with wanting it?
With knowing it is all there is.

Name something more important
and I promise you,
if you can
I will write that poem instead.

Falling

When you tried to catch me the first time,
I did not know how to be held.
I was too busy
trying to break down
another man's walls
to realize that you had
dropped yours voluntarily.
I didn't know it was
supposed to be that easy.
I did not know the value
of an honest man
until I was taxed by the
breath of a liar.
I could not see you clearly.
but reality is often
a remedy for innocence.
I cannot pretend to see
through the eyes
of a child anymore,
I am sorry it took so long.
Did I tell you how
he lied in the end?
Did I tell you how
he named me future
only to keep his past
as our present?
Did I tell you how
I became a woman
the day I finally
stopped reaching
for childish things?

He was a childish thing
I do not hope to punish you
for the half-truths of another,
but there are some lessons
we cannot unlearn.
I can no longer
afford to jump
with my eyes closed.
I have inspired music in you,
but will you still feel the same
when I am no longer a pursuit?
will I be less of a muse in your arms?
was I more beautiful
when you had to chase me?
See, I know the irony of men now.
when they finally get what they want
they do not know what to do with it.
seems they are more
in love with chasing the woman
than with keeping her.
how do you wear your manhood?
is it omnipresent
like oxygen,
or do you reach for it
only when you are in costume?
Most men,
wear their masculinity like mask.
a fragile thing;
to be worn only in the presence of other men.
I need to know yours is authentic.
that it will still be there
when I am the only one looking.
There are some things
I have never been able to say

41

off paper.
I am not yet fully comfortable
with being vulnerable out loud.
is that okay?
will you accept poems
when my throat stops working?
will you believe they are
the only way I know how
to be honest with the world?
How necessary is sleep?
when you share
a bed with a poet,
you will not be
a stranger to
sleepless nights.
or to pen strokes
in the dark.
I will often toss and turn, tormented.
Some poems are relentless that way.
are you as committed to them as I am?
Do you know what it looks like
when a woman needs to be held?
she will not ask for it.
if you listen,
her silence will always
tell you more than her words will.
are you listening?
How familiar are you with broken?
Will your hands
become beach pails
on the nights
I feel more like sand than rock?
Do you like roller coasters?
will you enjoy

the highs and lows of me,
or will you vomit
at the first sign of gravity?
I do not take you for a man
with the stomach of a boy,
but I could be wrong.
we both know
I have been wrong
so many times before.

There Will Be Poems

If you are to date a poet, be forewarned;
there will be poems.
seems obvious enough, but many men
find it surprising when they come so quickly;
the poems, that is.
The poems are always a source of confusion.
The first few, will always mention
flutter by moments, a mouth full of sugar,
and goosebumped flesh.
Their metaphors will be wrapped tightly in hope.
These will be the poems you will want to remember.
Rejoice in them.
Let them roll around on your tongue.
so you can savor their sticky sweet taste.
give them a home in your memory
and repeat them back to us when we forget
why we wrote them.
There will be days we forget why we wrote them.
The poems that follow will expose you
in a way you did not sign up for.
Nothing will be too sacred. not your mother, your
childhood, or your birthmark.
we will try to piece you together.
build you up, so we can tear you down; line by line.
we will find connections you never knew were there.
we will turn them into a stanza .we will turn you into a
metaphor.
A room full of strangers
will know what your sex tastes like;
we will tell them how you made us cum
they will know the smell of your orgasm

before they even know your name.
As time goes by,
and poems pile up you will find the ones
that reveal the most will not recall the way
our bodies dance in summer sweat,
or the way your fingers whisper spells
on to the surface of my skin.
They won't even be the ones
that make mockery of your manhood.
you will feel most violated
by the poems we write about ourselves.
you will watch us give away our softest parts
willingly to an audience
and you will recall the warfare in our eyes
when you first asked for our name.
you will recall the moments of silence between us
and you will not understand
how I so easily surrender myself
to a notebook and a room full of strangers,
only to deadbolt the lock on my secrets in front of you.
our most intimate moments will no longer belong to us;
and you will not know how to feel about this.
accept it. accept me.
I will release those moments to a room full of ears
because I was not given another way
to make sense of things.
you will need to learn
to embrace the poem you have become;
we are a poem now.
you will be on stage even when you aren't.
Find comfort behind the mic
and warmth beneath these bright lights
make home of these listeners;
and if ever you feel I am detached,

you can always find me in my notebook.

Love: In *There will be poems*, I warn a lover what it will be like to love a poet. Write a letter to the next person who will fall in love with you. What do they have to look forward to? What should they be careful of? Is there anything you could say now that can prepare them for the adventure ahead? What should they know?

Heartbreak.

"Nobody's going to save you.
No one's going to cut you down,
cut the thorns thick around you.
No one's going to storm the
castle walls, nor kiss awake your
birth, climb down your hair,
nor mount you onto the white
steed. There is no one who will
feed the yearning. Face it. You
will have to do it yourself."

-Gloria Anzaldua

When your heart
is handed back to you

When your heart
is handed back to you,
do not look down at it.
Do not squeeze it
or throw it on the floor
or step on it with angry feet.
Do not lose your mind
or try to make him lose his.
Do not throw it back at him
Hoping he will catch it
He won't
His palms are not even big enough
to hold his own.
When your heart
is handed back to you,
Do not put it in the freezer.
Do not hold it your warm hands
and watch the condensation
create a puddle for it to swim in.
Do not stand there; numb
eyes wide and lips parted
Hoping he will change his mind He won't.
Do not make a fool of yourself.
He will already have done that for you.
He will have already stolen
the diamonds from your eyes
and used them to replace
the stars that framed the black sky above
New York City
the night he gave himself

to someone else.
I am paralyzed
By the idea of your hands
on her skin.
The thought of her body
imitating mine
beneath yours-
makes me desire the fires of hell.
The idea of her mouth
exploring places
I made my own
makes me want
to disappear.

The thought of her name
replacing mine on your tongue
made me want to see my own blood.

And so I did.
cried violently
as it ran ambitiously
in the rain like you did
in the LA marathon.

At last finding peace
in the stillness of sleep
as it rested on my thighs
and dried into the fabric
of my clothes.

Things to Keep in Mind
When Your Heart is Broken

It's called a break-up, because it's broken.

You cannot make him stay.

You shouldn't want to.
Even if you could-
the best parts of your relationship
will forever be lost in his desire to exit, anyway.

When he is ready to leave, help him pack.
hold the door wide open and let him go.
Anything more than this will only prolong the
inevitable. He is already gone.
You will miss him.
be kind to yourself when you do.
it is normal to resort to auto-pilot.
Normal, for every street in this city
to scream his name at you.
For every piece of furniture
in your apartment to feel like marked territory.
At night, everything you own
will shapeshift into a reminder of his absence.

It is always easier to leave than it is to be left.
Even if he is hurting too,
his process won't be anything like yours.

Do not torture yourself.
in the weeks following a break-up
listening to Adele is not "therapy"-

it is self-inflicted torture.
cruel and unusual punishment, at best.
you have been warned.

No matter how carefully worded
your Facebook status is,
or how much fun you **look**
like you're having on Instagram-
he is not going to call you.

This is a good thing.

When the phone does ring,
any voice on the other end that does not belong to him
will seem foreign to you.
Irrelevant, even.
His, will be the only one you want to hear.
The only one that moves you.

Ignoring people who **are** calling
to spend time thinking
about people who *aren't*, makes no sense.

Answer the phone.
When your friends ask you how you are,
answer honestly.
There is no strength in pretending.
It is okay not to be okay.

If your heart hurts, it still works.
There is no shame in feeling,
hurting only makes you more human, and growth can
only come from being honest with yourself.

No one can take from you
what you haven't already given them, willingly.
You are allowed to take it all back
if ever they begin to mistreat it.

There are many things in this life
that you will never fully comprehend.
Love is only one them.
No matter how many tears or bottles of wine you invest,
it is a waste of time
trying to make sense of senseless things

There is *nothing* time can't fix.
Take comfort in this.

Forgiveness is a life skill.
Just because he didn't love you the way you wanted,
doesn't mean he didn't love you with everything he had.
Forgive him, for not having enough. Forgive
yourself, for always offering too much.

What no one ever tells you about love,
is that it's not always enough.

When all is said and done, do not mistake yourself for
anything pathetic. You are no one's victim.
You are a work in progress.
Wear this heartbreak the way you have all the others;
Proof, that you will still be able to love with reckless
abandon. Even after you are left feeling reckless and
abandoned. Yours is a warrior heart.

This... is a good thing.

The Shape of your Back

I have memorized the shape of your back;
The way your footsteps
sound walking opposite my direction,
I could pick out the back of your head
in a crowded room;
What is it about me
that always makes you want to leave?
I ask myself too often questions
I already know the answers to.
I cannot claim to know love personally;
Cannot pretend I've seen it before,
But I do know it must not look like this:
Like leaving,
must not sound like
broken promises or confusion;
like, "I do...just not right now"
 I imagine that real love looks hard.
Solid. Like concrete. Unmistakable,
Like the sound of laughter.
Hard as I try, I cannot seem
to find the logic in loving someone
who is so often curious about the color
of the grass on the other side,
 But here I am again.
My eyes on your back,
Fighting back tears,
Too proud to say a word,
But not *'proud enough'*
to forbid you
from coming back next week.
Funny; how I always let you *leave,*

But never *let you go.*
Senseless acts of love
Never go unpunished.
as if I lent you my heart And you forgot to give it back;
As if it were something insignificant
I left in your car one day; Like sunglasses,
Or lip gloss…a hair tie.
I imagine it sits beating inside your glove box,
waiting patiently for you to get around to it
     …and I hope you do soon.
I cannot keep filling
this void in my chest with poems.
Cannot keep letting my inbox
overflow with messages
from boys who couldn't
even matter to me if they tried.
Cannot keep hoping
that each message back *to them*
will somehow
lessen the sting of *your* absence.
it never does.
Look, I just want to laugh
the way I did before I met you:
Full. Whole.
I just want to wear my smile
the way I used to
before you made it yours.
And even though I should by now
I still Don't Know How
I hope I do not Love this way
Forever; Painful.
Always trying to keep things
that simply do not want to be kept

57

Death of the forest
Inspired by Jasmine Wilkerson Sufi

I remember the day we planted the seeds
how it wasn't long before the stems grew
thick, fast, and strong around us.

People watched.
marveled at our green thumbs.
Trees grew tall and wise.
We secured tire swings,
Put up wind chimes,
Built our house beneath the shade,
we feasted on the fruits
that blossomed above us.
We made a home of that forest.

But this marrowless bone
salvaged from the mangled
corpse that became of us...
this orphan branch is all that is left.
This lifeless limb
is the only proof I have
that a forest once stood here.

For too long these bloody fingertips
have held on to it so hopeful.
heart wrenching;
the way they caress the peeling bark
like the cold skin of a dead child
a desperate mother insists is just sleeping.
I have over stayed my welcome
Believing myself a martyr

Believing that staying and waiting
will make a good story one day
One, that maybe we will share
at PTA meetings and dinner parties
I would say, that I always knew
he was coming back
He would laugh and reply
"How could I ever stay away?"
and he would kiss me
The way he used to.
Like a trophy that *almost* didn't belong to him-
the way he did when he loved me.
For too long I believed he was coming back
Even though when he left
he said, **he was not coming back.**

For too long I have been a fleeting memory
begging to be remembered
a dead language desperate to be spoken
a woman determined
to be held by balled up fists

For too long I have been a cremated body
begging not to be a pile of ashes anymore.

I do not want to be a pile of ashes anymore.
But the truth is everything we were
can be reduced to a pile of ashes now
The house. The swing. The fruit. The wind chime.
The whole damn forest.
We made ashes of it all.

And I, like a deranged pioneer
sit alone panning in the river

long after the gold has been rushed
and all the men have gone home-
I am committed to finding something,
anything, to hold on to.
And I always do.
you always find what you never stop seeking.
even if it means you have to create it for yourself.
a woman determined to stay
can make a reason to out of anything.

the silence between us can transform
into a list of ways we are just like
Romeo and Juliet-
star crossed lovers separated by circumstance
but still in love all the same.

I have sat atop these ashes for too long now.
mourning and ready to rebuild

sat here staring at the ruins
but I see now that the forest had to be destroyed
so that I could see the horizon more clearly.

I cannot keep living like the word
that is always waiting to fill in your blanks.
I am not a bookmark.
My name means infinite.
I am a daughter of the Sun.
Chosen by my ancestors.
I hold in this womb the strength of every
w o m a n who has ever lived.
She guides me now with the compass
of wisdom she placed in my chest
She has shown me

what it means to search for what matters;
and now I am finding myself in the clouds.

I see now that I am the one
I have been waiting for.
I am the one:
The firework. The beloved.
The red lipped, open mouthed,
fist in the air, long haired,
heart in her hand, warrior woman.

It has always been me.
I see that now.
I am searching for me now.
and when I find myself,
the search will be over.
For when I find **myself,**
I need not look for anyone else.

Throwing Away His Toothbrush

Throwing away his toothbrush
means you are no longer
hoping he will come home.
It means
you are no longer his home.
When you throw away his toothbrush-
you are ready to write the poems.
Which is to say;
when you throw away his toothbrush-
you are ready to let him go.
There is no way to un live the past
and once they are written
there is no way to un write the poems.
They will live far longer than you do.
They will reach further than your hope did.
They will do as they always have:
they will serve as a bridge.
a place to find salvation
from the raging river of your pain
a place to rest on the long journey home.
But to find it,
you must throw away his toothbrush
and trust that will be enough
to dislodge the words
that have been stuck
in your hopeful heart
for far longer than they needed to be.

In the End,

when the last bits of me have lost all their flavor
and I am nothing more than a forgettable trace
of an old stick of gum
stuck to the bottom of your shoe,
The women
will be there
to scrape
me off.

The women have always outlived the men in my life.
The women have always out loved the men in my life.

This is the only way we survive;
by scraping one another
off the soles of wing tipped male egos
and molding each other back
into something recognizable;
just
one
more
time.

"Your leaving says nothing
about what is left...
I am blooming, my love.
Even after you have chosen
not to watch."

-Yesika Salgado

Heartbreak: Describe the room you were in the last time you got your heart broken. What did you hear? see? smell? Describe the moment you realized the other person fell out of love with you. Did they tell you directly or did they tell you through their actions?

_____

_____

_____

_____

_____

_____

_____

_____

_____

_____

_____

_____

_____

_____

_____

_____

_____

Death.

January 20th

On January 20th I turned 23.
 Around 4 o'clock that day,
I walked into my dad's room
to find him lying on the floor barely conscious;
clothes wet with urine,
he was too weak to make it to the bathroom...
I guess.

I was alone.
as I dialed 911, time stopped.
The words fell out of my mouth
like razor blades
watched the ambulance
race in slow motion. backward even.
my father had refused
a liver transplant a long time ago
and had been dying ever since.
seems I was the last one to know.
I spent my birthday in the hospital.

He was gone four days later.
It is now almost a year later
and I have yet to shatter
like I know I am supposed to.
Until we finally let him go,
I never understood
that you are never fully human
until you've experienced yourself
at your most broken.
I remember wanting
to become part of the floor that night.

I spread myself on to the ground
wet and hollow,
the same way my tears did.
In that moment,
*every*thing had changed.

I went home. Sunk into the couch,
and never wanted to breathe the same way again.
All I felt, were deep waves of pain.
followed by loud silence.
Words lost meaning. saw no point in necessities
like showers or food. I was numb.
what use did a shell of a person
have for everyday things anyway?
Saying "no one prepares you for this"
is an understatement.

No one told me
I'd feel empty and meaningless
like conversations with strangers.
No one said I'd feel guilty for laughing.
No one told me
that from this point forward,
my father would be the bruise behind my smile,
the thing I would have for the rest of my life
to compare all of my problems to,
my defining tragedy.
and since then,
drops from the ocean of my pain
will leak on to paper every once in a while;

but for the most part,
I fear that I have too much in common
with the levies of Katrina.

My face, a wall of "I'm okay."
My insides, a wrecking ball of
"no... you're not"
I still do not know
where I am supposed to
put all of this pain.
So I wear it heavy,
the only way I know how: Silent.
the way most pain tends to torture.
I guess,
we do what we know
before we know what to do.
and so I fake it.
the weight this deserves
is too heavy to bare all at once.
So I fill the void with poetry,
and people, and places,
there is *always* somewhere to go.

Can't sit with myself for too long,
maybe I know what that will mean.

Maybe, I hate the silence now.
or maybe I need it.
Either way,
I guess some poems fight to exist.
I know this one did.

To the Daughters Who Will Lose Their Fathers Too Soon

Daughter of death, prepare yourself.
you must welcome your tears in place of him;
they will keep you safe now.
you are going to speak of tears
more often than you ever thought possible.
You will hate them, and need them,
and wish their well would dry up;
they will come heavy at first. Heavy and hard;
uncontrollable, even.
your body will shake
even when you tell it to stop.
This will scare you.
Then one day,
It will be quiet in the still of a March night,
and they will stop coming for a while.
when they return they will show up like death did;
Inconvenient.
They will burn.
Like your insides have frozen over
and the only way to cry now
is to release shards of jagged ice
from your tear ducts that cut the flesh
of your face on their way down
to kiss the tiles of restaurants
and classrooms and kitchens.
Yes, They will burn like that.
but you will need them.
There will be nothing else you can do.
Your chest will burn too.
Sometimes for no reason at all,

but mostly out of anger.
One day, you will see a little girl and her father
in the airport and you will stare at them holding hands.
You will stare until the tears come.
and you will have to convince yourself not to walk over.
You will want to warn her that her hands
will not be small enough to fit into the palms of his
forever,
and to hold on to them as long as she can.
But you won't.
You will only stare.
and you will find that you stare too long
at everything these days.
Not only at little girls and their fathers
in airports but at anything that reminds you
that yours is gone.
You will feel sad even when you are happy
and you will say you are okay
when you are really not.
friends, will think it is okay to leave you alone,
and this is when the tears will come.
This is when they must.
you will be right when you start to feel
like nothing is the same and no one understands.
This is because nothing will be the same
and because no one will understand.
They Can't.
You cannot describe how it felt
when your chest caved in,
so they cannot know
what it will feel like when you are convinced
your heart has stopped beating.
Your friends, will get to know another person.
one who feels pain at the slightest jog of a memory;

one who lives with her spirit drenched in death.
This will be hard for them to watch.
They will not know what to do.
they will tell you not to let your father
take you with him;
but you will think that he already has.

They will sometimes need to convince you
that you are still breathing,
and that life is not a broken plate.
Sometimes you will believe them,
sometimes you won't.
 Do not feel obligated to remain in one piece.
You will smile again when your face remembers
how. and this is okay.
This will be okay
for as long as you need it to be.
 Settle into your pain. Bite down, Chew it,
and let it digest until it has become part
of the person you are becoming.
You will need to find ways
to do this for the rest of your life.
you will have questions. This is okay too.
You will not be sure you know how to mourn,
so you will ask if you are doing it right.
But the answer will always be: yes.
You will want to know where he is
and where he went;
you will be unsettled about that.
But the answer will always be: to rest.
You will get angry and ask why
he wasn't there to see you graduate,
why he won't walk you down the aisle,
or be there to nickname your children

and the answer will always be:
he was, and he will be.
He will be there if you are.
In your laugh that sounds like his,
in the mariachi trumpets
in your throat when you sing,
in all your tasteless jokes,
and in every burning tear
you let drop down
to kiss the ground in his honor;
I promise.
He will be there, if you are.

Dear Daddy

I'm sorry I don't miss you enough
At least not enough out loud.
No one gets it.
I'm sorry I get distracted with things
that matter so much less than you.
I'm sorry I cry at night and get angry at you for leaving
me. I know it wasn't your fault.
I'm sorry
That When I am forced to sit through
A father-daughter dance,
I am sorry I feel like
Dying.
Sometimes I think
having you back would solve everything.
Maybe then it wouldn't hurt so much.
Maybe then I wouldn't feel so empty.
Maybe then I would look forward to Thanksgiving again
instead of dreading it.
So you could tell jokes,
and my mom could roll her eyes at you.
And me and my sisters could laugh
and eat. and laugh, and eat.
But it's just us, now.
and I wish I could say that is enough,
but it's not. It's just not.
Sometimes I just want my Daddy.
I just want you to call me
for no reason at all
just to say you're proud of me.
Even when I haven't done
anything worth being proud of.

In so many ways,
I am still waiting for that phone call.
I don't think
I will ever stop waiting.

I am in love now.
With a man who shares your spirit.
He wants to have a family with me.
Says I would be an amazing mother,
Wants us to build an empire.
But it scares me to think
my children will never know your voice.
I get sad on Saturdays
when the Sun is out
and the sky is clear
I can still see you pulling up
with your oldies blasting,
combing your mustache,
and yelling
"Mija, look at the sky!
it's a beautiful day. You want some menudo?
Let's go cruising."
I get sad when I have nothing to fill the silence,
and these days, that is often.
I just want to hug you again.
To hear your voice again.
To be with you
In the most serious of moments;
just to hear you ruin it
One last time
by making a joke.
I just miss you, daddy.
And there is no poetic way to say that.

I try so hard to remember you.
To wear green often,
and share your proverbs
with my students.
I even talk like you.
& point out
flawed logic
whenever I get the chance-
I try my hardest to
carry you in my spirit,
but sometimes
it just isnt enough.

Sometimes,
nothing
is.

"The only way to keep what I have gained; my gratitude and the spiritual principals that I understand today, is to give them away to another human being. My concern is not what that human being does with it. But my hope is that he will get hope and that he will change his life by seeing an example."

-Ernesto Aguirre
1947-2011

Death: You may or may not know what it is like to lose someone you love, but we can all relate to the fact that one day we will die. Picture yourself on your death bed. How old are you? Who is around? What kinds of things have people brought to try and make you smile? What are your last words of wisdom you want to leave your loved ones with?

_____

_____

_____

_____

_____

_____

_____

_____

_____

_____

_____

_____

_____

_____

_____

_____

Growth.

"Why am I compelled to write?...
Because the world I create in the writing
compensates for what the real world does
not give me. By writing I put order in the
world, give it a handle so I can grasp it...
To discover myself, to preserve myself, to
make myself, To convince myself that I am
worthy and that what I have to say is not a
pile of shit... Finally I write because I'm
scared of writing, but I'm more scared of
not writing."

— Gloria Anzaldua

A Letter to Myself at 14

I know how small the world seems.
I know it feels like this is all there is
like there is nothing more important than this moment
but I have to warn you, you are not really living.
Living and existing are two different things.
This is not love.
I know you are longing for someone to hold on to.
I know that your daddy never really told you this,
but love is not supposed to hurt.
I promise you are too young
to know the difference, but this is not love.
It is insanity.
He does not love you. He is sick and twisted and
because he was born with no life in his chest
He will try to take yours.
Pay attention.
The first time he gives you a glimpse of his demon,
 It will be on the phone.
He will be upset with you for going to a party
without asking him first- you will apologize.
you like him, so you will mistake this for affection.
you are so young, you will accept it.
Welcome it, even.
you will think this is the way a boy asks you
 to belong to him but you will be wrong.
This, is not the beginning. It is the end.
Beware. This warning sign. red flag.
This fluorescent blinking light begging you to
Stop and turn back now. You are not a possession.
Not a thing to be owned.
You belong to no one not even to yourself yet-

you are only 14.
You cannot give away something
you have not yet grown into.
The first time he hits you you will think you deserve it
you will have spent so much time isolated
that normal will be relative.
Logic will no longer live here.
in your life. He will give you rules:
no more church. no more friends. no talking back.
or cussing. last and most important:
you are never to speak to another man.
not even to say thank you in a restaurant.
The last one will be the hardest to follow.
You will blame your parents for this.
for them drilling manners into your habits.
Taught you to be polite.
To always say "thank you" Not knowing the
Consequences this would one day have on their
daughter's lower back in the form of a rug burn.
you will keep your mouth shut.
Continue living two lives; checking in
every two hours but only from your house phone
cell phones move too easy
One day you will accidentally forget to wear shorts
underneath your skirt.
This will cause him
to bruise your face for the very first time.
By then, you will be very good at hiding bruises
and bite marks on arms and thighs and wrists
but there is no wearable garment
that can cover a purple jaw
.no believable excuse readily available for the cut
beneath your eye.
"I fell" can only work so many times.

84

How often can one person fall?
No one is that clumsy. Not even you.
You will hate him for making it public.
For exposing you: pathetic
For making you wear your weakness
across your face.
For showing the world you have no backbone.
Babygirl, You will feel helpless. like a sail boat
in a hurricane. Do not let him do this to you.
You were born a lion.
Do not let him make a mouse of you.
Do not let him rob you of your God.
If you let him, he will take away your shine
and it will take you years to get it back.
and even when you do
it will not be the same.
Dimmer, it will flicker
on and off sometimes.
Hold tight to who you are
Do not let him shame you of your art.
Do not make yourself smaller to fit into his world.
His world is not somewhere you want to be,
It is cold there. lonely. and scary. dangerous at night.
Everyone is afraid all the time
and the women there are not allowed
to make any noise.
They think this is the way
love is supposed to feel.
But they are wrong.
They don't know any better.
Babygirl, I promise-
Love does not empty you.
It does not make you
contemplate suicide.

It does not silence you.
Or force you to push away
the people you love,
It does not ask you to lie to them.
It will not laugh at your dreams
or tell you that you are not going to college
It will not rip up your sample applications
Or your nephew's baby pictures.
Love does not intimidate.
It does not smash things
or sock walls just to show you how hard it can hit.
It does not make you miserable.
Love does not peel away the layers of your identity or
eat away at your not yet developed self-esteem.
It does not leave you lifeless.
I am trying to show you the ugliest parts of this
to scare your feet into flight.
hoping these will be the things that will save you from
this. But only you can do that.
Only you can take back the things he took from you by
not giving them to him in the first place.
But I already know that you won't.
This letter is 10 years too late-
you are only 14 and stubborn. and want so badly to be
loved that you will accept the first offer you get. No
matter how hard it hits.
I am sorry. You will spend 3 years as a prisoner of a war
you never meant to fight
3 years wishing you were not so pathetic
3 years in preparation
Experiencing over and over and over again
exactly what love is not
so that when it finally shows up
ready and willing like a brand new beginning
You will recognize it for the victory that it is.

86

Nazerenes Don't Dance

I was a Christian once.
Vaguely remember being religious
but I will never forget Ecuador.
At 14, I would have told you
I had been 'called' to become a missionary.
quoted bible verses,
then described (in detail)
Why I felt I had been 'called'
to the Equator to spread the word
of a god I barely knew.
There I was. Trying to convince the indigenous
On another continent; that MY truth was theirs too,
 Built them a church with a state of the art
Sound system in a town on a hill
In Quito, covered with tin roofed shacks full of
hospitality.
So self-righteous we were.
Posing for pictures, buying souvenirs,
pretending this trip was for them.
our sympathy would end when our trip did.
Our jobs done, Church built; People recruited,
mission accomplished.
And I, 12 days later would land back at LAX;
My mind, once closed with belief,
now open wide with wonder.
I had come back from a place and a people,
 too beautiful and perfect as they already were;
not to be ashamed of myself
upon arrival back home.
 As missionaries, We were told this mission
would strengthen our relationship with god,

Make us better Christians, help us better serve the lord.
But I remember the last words said to me as a Christian.
My arm outstretched, being pulled toward a friendship
circle by a little Ecuadorian girl in the rainforest,
My pastor said:
"Angie, no. We're *Nazerene*. Nazerenes don't dance."
and with that, I set the tone for the rest of my life:
I danced anyway.
As I spun and laughed
Like a beautiful tornado,
I was finally free.
I had found the mission
within the mission of my mission trip.
We, pretending to know who god was,
Told them THEY had the wrong idea;
used the word "saved" so often in our sales pitch
You would think we knew what it meant
How dare us.
I won't pretend to know about yours;
But MY experience with religion has taught me that the
religious are never satisfied.
Too busy pointing out the holes in each other's fables,
never let the beautiful stay that way.
Refuse to see the perfection in the different;
The blind leading the deaf;
trying to sell an impossible certainty to one another.
Always trying to "fix" people,
Somehow convinced that they,
themselves, are not broken.

Confessions of a Drunk Driver

I was released around noon.
I stood at the back door of the Pasadena Jail
with all of my belongings in a clear plastic bag.
I remember seeing my mom's car across the street.in my
head, I begged her to make that u-turn faster,
I felt like everyone I'd ever known
were in the passing cars
Staring at me in disgust,
like they knew what I had done.
The first place my mother took me
was back to where I crashed.
On the way I sat in the backseat
more silent than I knew I was capable of being
I traced the skid marks
on the freeway with my eyes.
seemed they were 24 years long.
I kept tracing until they led me to cracked pavement.
A broken curb, what used to be a stop sign,
and a mutilated fence.
My car stopped just 5 feet from the overpass
Your life looks a hell of a lot clearer
In the light of day.
She made me get out of the car.
ironic, it was the same spot
I had refused the breathalyzer
just hours before
convinced I wasn't drunk-
silence. she told me to stand there.
to soak in this moment. this pain. this mistake.
My eyeslids heavy with shame,
she told me to keep them open

in a voice I'd never heard before.
I hurt her growing up, but not like this.
never like this.
"I almost lost my baby" she said.
I said nothing.
couldn't even look at her.
angry and heartbroken,
"you know it was you're daddy who saved you, right?"
 I stood there until I was only bones.
"If you still don't believe in god little girl, now would be a
damn good time to start."
I hung my head. sorrow and regret
eat away at flesh easily.
The truth is, I did not know how to write this poem.
This is the one that has terrorized me.
the one that will not let me sleep.
the one I am living every single day.
because I chose it that way.
Although I did not happen
to claim any lives that night;
it should not have taken a DUI,
2 years probation, a totaled car,
an AB541 class,
135 hours of community service
and over $1400 in fines
and city property damage
to realize I can't control my drinking.

This poem is not an apology for who I am,
it is an apology
for who I was willing
to become that night.
It's an apology to my mother my father
my sister to Molly for being so godamn selfish.

as if driving drunk was a risk that would only affect me
It's an apology to Donny and Natalie and Venessa
and to everyone else
who tried to tell me I had a drinking problem.
shit, its even an apology to that fence,
for having to give its life so that I could keep mine.
This poem is an apology to Joss,
who lost her mother to a drunk driver
when she was only 16
She now spends her time sharing her story
in DUI classes trying to help people like me
see that there are consequences
of their unwritten poems.
She is one of them.
This poem, is everything I am too ashamed
to be out loud.
a pathetic attempt at redemption,
a message to anyone who needs it.
an apology to everyone I've hurt,
myself included-by not dealing with this sooner.
and last but not least,
it's an apology to anyone reading this;
because you,
just as easily could've been that fence.

And I am sorry.

I wonder if I am crazy

I am as much a lover
as I am a fighter
and he knows this to be true.
In the same breath
I use to beg him to stay-
I will curse his name.
spew fire in his direction
and make known
my lion's roar.
I am fickle this way.
I fear I will never
learn the art of restraint.
Fear that I will never be anything
like what he thought
he would want-
A woman
Too much like
The worst of his memories.
Sometimes I wonder
If I am crazy.
Wonder if there are times
my Skin has chameleoned itself
into a transparent film
Draping my bones,
And my insides are revealed
For all the world to see.
I have wondered this
too many times
for it not to be true.
Trust me.
I don't imagine

That most people live like this;
Questioning their balance this often.
I do not think
it is common to
w o n d e r
whether or not
You are a threat
to the people you love the most
I imagine most people do not feel like explosives.
like holy science experiments
Or rough drafts-
created carelessly
but turned in anyway.
Like an essay written on the way to class
Ignoring all the grammatical errors
and simple misspellings-
Or a poem
always finished
at the very last minute,
Nowhere near it's potential-
But posted anyway.
Because
it is April.
and the crops
are coming in all around you;
and you -
standing around
Watching the genius bloom-
are tired of only harvesting.
You too,
have seeds of your own
that are ready to be sewn,
you too are a poet
Even though it is sometimes easy to forget.

If there is a God, this is for you.

Hi, I know we haven't talked in a while...
Or maybe I just haven't talked back.
Maybe, I just don't know what to say.
I mean, even if I tried to reply
most of my prayers would be questions anyway,
Is that okay?
Like, what am I doing here?
is there even a point?
Like why did you give me
this desire to create,
and then make me into
someone who always feels so inadequate?
Why did you let my father die?
Didn't you know I would need him?
Didn't you know you would leave this hole in my heart
that nothing would be able to fill?
Why did you do that?
Does he still ask about me?
...Is it okay that I am angry with you?
Is that allowed?
Is that the reason you have
been keeping my poems from me?
When will I get them back?
Will they be the same when I do?
I don't understand so many things.
Why is everything so hard for me?
Can't even pay the bills without
getting confused and frustrated,
How am I supposed to figure out if you exist?
Am I asking too many questions?
Why do I have to take medicine?

Why does the world like me better when I do?

Why do I feel so empty all the time?
Even when my heart and lungs are full,
and my body is resting in the arms of a man
who loves me sacrificially,
Something is missing.
And I know it might be you,
But I don't know how to ask you to come back.
I refuse to call you
by any name I've ever heard before.
I refuse to follow a trend.
To be a sheep in a leaderless heard,
I don't want to go to church.
The people are faceless there.
I want to find you again in my poems.
In a room full of people
hungry for the truth.
I want you to feed them through me,
like the prophet I know I was born to be
but I cannot do that without my words, god.
Give them back.
I no longer feel at home
in the house of give and take,
I have lost my way.
You spoke to me through my love last night,
but I couldn't make out your voice.
It was muffled.
Caught somewhere between my ego
and his broad perception of what you are,
I was listening
but I heard nothing.
Only your knocking.

But I had no idea how to open the door.

I am lost.
In so many ways.
I often feel misguided.
Left for dead,
Alone.
In a world that is waiting for me to fail.

but I am not a people pleaser.
Never have been,
and I do not want to start today.

I know I am capable of more.
I just don't know if I can bridge the gap
between mediocrity
and greatness.

Talking about it
is a whole lot harder
than being about it.
and I want to.
I just don't know how.
And that is the truth.

I no longer think I can do it all alone.
But I think that's where you come in.
Whoever you are.
Whatever your name is,
I need you now.
I am starving for truth
and I don't have the
tools to feed myself anymore,
I know that know.

I humble myself before you,
And I ask that you look for me again.
Just one more time.

Don't give up on me yet,
There is so much more work to do.
...Write back soon.
I will be looking for the signs,
I promise to keep my heart,
eyes, and ears, wide open.

Help me reach my fullest potential,
and please give me my poems back.

Thanks, and...sorry this took so long.

Ps.
Say hi to my dad for me.
and tell him I'm doing my best to get it all right.

Love,
Angie

Growth: The truth is I am in a constant state of growth. As you can tell by the poems in this section, I still have a lot of growing up to do. What about you? What areas of your life have you grown in or need to grow from? Take this time to reflect on your own growth. Begin with the line "I may not be where I want to be, but thank God I'm not where I was"

_____

_____

_____

_____

_____

_____

_____

_____

_____

_____

_____

_____

_____

_____

_____

_____

Womanhood.

"I will no longer be made to feel
ashamed of existing. I will have my
voice: Indian, Spanish, white.
I will have my serpent's tongue –
my woman's voice, my sexual voice,
my poet's voice.
I will overcome the tradition of
silence."

-Gloria Anzaldua

On Being a Woman

What do men know of war?
Of lipstick and land mines
Of contingency plans;
plotting and plucking
straightening and strategies.
High heels and hostility.
What do men know of surrender?
Of giving up before all is destroyed
What do they know of sacrifice?
Of letting him eat first
Of giving him the bigger piece
Of being taught the width of his stomach is somehow
wider than yours.

What do men know of hunger?

Of watching him devour the last slice
pretending like you didn't want it -
Knowing it is not lady-like to want
anything but him.

You are allowed to want
e v e r y thing AND him.
You are more than safety net hands;

But no one ever tells us that, do they?

Women and Wolves

wild women and wolves
are made of the same magic.
creatures of instinct;
fierce and enigmatic.
both labeled dangerous.
and made to feel ashamed of being what they are.
endangered;
watching our kind disappear
into the torture of captivity.
into the torment of white walls.
our ancestors did not understand walls when they
came for us.
we tried to devour them but they swallowed us first.
we did not ask to be saved.
we were beings of light and nature
we knew only how to be led
by the compass in our chests but were told to ignore it
when they put us in a dress.
this was a foreign thing.
they called it rescue.
said we should thank them.
taught us to be polite.
to use our inside-voices. to be lady-like
means to quiet the growls
to silence the hunger pains of a starved soul
only silence is acceptable from women inside walls.
sound is for the wild. it belongs outdoors.
sound is a savage thing.
something to be tamed like women.
and wolves.
but we do not belong to walls.

103

we are daughters of the sun,
we belong only to light and choice.
There is something
so primitive in the way we know.
we are the most beautiful
of feral things;
 we must stop pretending to be so civilized.
pretending we still don't crave the wander.
the desire to roam has not left us,
it has instead been re-named
restless. unstable.unpredictable.
these are not lady-like things.
it is not lady like to want, only to give.
but the song of a starved soul sounds a lot like howling
at the moon;
we are howling at the moon.

can you hear us?

Boobs vs. Brains

I was once asked by an administrator
In college what my major was.
"Rhetoric" I answered
in my cut off jean shorts and crop top.
Rhetoric.
The art of using language
to communicate effectively.
Through condescending eyes,
he looked at me as if I'd just
told him a joke he didn't quite get.
Through a half-curled smile
and a vacant attempt
at holding back a laugh
 "rhetoric??" he said loudly-
"I would have guessed ...fashion"
Then, stumbling over his words
I continued to look at him sideways
he continued, digging a deeper hole,
"I ...just figured, such a pretty girl
would be interested in more ...feminine things"
and I stopped myself. I could have lunged at him.
I could have grabbed the envelope opener
off of his desk, held it to his throat,
allowed the words to run up from mine.
jump out of my mouth at him and say:
"What the HELL is THAT supposed to mean?"
but I didn't.
I simply stood there in passive compliance,
And let him finish signing off on my grad check.
I've always been told:
You don't bite the hand that feeds you.

What you DO is: wait until you're full
and then, you burn down the fucking kitchen.

so I asked him for clarification:
"what exactly do you mean by feminine?"
And the details of his answer
are about as relevant as his identity.
he had no idea what he meant.
The intentions of that comment
were probably lost somewhere between
sexism and a pathetic attempt
at trying to hit on someone half his age.
Not being taken seriously at first glance
is something I've dealt with my whole life:
girls like me
are often expected to be just that.
and nothing more.
but contrary to first glance,
I have always been more "brains" than "boobs."
Men like him have taught me
that expectations are sharp,
Which is why I am always out to prove a point:
The same men who wouldn't think twice
About **looking** at us in lust
would second guess themselves
Before they ever actually **listen**
to what we have to say.
The problem with that is:
I've always been a little larger
than the average woman;
so their expectations never quite fit me,
They were always too small.
See, I wear my womanhood proud;
I wear it ball gown, lipstick, mascara, and blush.

Do not ask me to tone that down,
so that **your** life can make more sense.
I will not be *less me* so that you can feel more
comfortable being *more you*.
I will not play small to serve you or your assumptions
of what hobbies I "should" have simply because
you happen to find me attractive.

As women, we are given two options:
Smart or beautiful
But the idea that femininity equates
to the absence of critical thinking skills
is nothing more than a delusion
conjured up by men
who are threatened by our ability to
BALANCE THE TWO.

As women, we OWN the right to be fly;
Patent is no longer pending- We **invented** the concept.
It is how we rule, how we write, and how we live:
Graceful. Like the wind in our hair.
Fierce. Like single mothers.
We are the iron fists in the silk gloves,
The AK-47's plated in gold,
we are grenades that explode
with the scent of cocoa butter.
We harness, **equal to men,**
the amount of strength needed
to either rebuild mankind;
or keep it sobbing
and begging for mercy,
on its knees before us.
The only difference is: when WE go to war,
we make the shit look good.

107

When She Brings the Wind

When she brings the wind
from the cyclone in her chest and throat-
you will be sorry.

you will wish you had made better choices.
you will wish your choices had made *you* better.
but it will be too late.

When she brings the wind
from the hell fire of her heavy heart,
it will be an untamed power you could not prepare for.
a power you cannot see
and one, you cannot ignore.

oh, when she brings the wind-
you will be sorry.

Giants will cower, using their languid limbs
to shield their fragile windows.
The giants know something you don't-
that even tempered glass
is no match for the savage in her weather.
The giants are careful. They know to tread lightly.
For when anger stirs in her
she inhales the forest, spits out a storm.
and everyone is sorry.
She is fury. blizzard and boiling point.
The ethereal voice that soothes us
with a purplepink sky just before she strikes.
Divine and dangerous,
her name is daughter, hurricane.

sister, tsunami. mother, monsoon.
grand mother, nature.
She is ex, wife and girlfriend.
Her name belongs to every woman
ever left for another.
any woman ever made
to freeze her thirst quenching rain
into fist sized hail-
Forced to transform,
so that she may remind mortal men
not to test the limits of her power.

I do not wish to die whole

When I am old
I do not wish to die whole.
I hope that by then
I will have given so freely of myself
that there will be nothing left to mourn.
Nothing to cry for.
Only a body
With skin weathered
and brown;
Tough-like the wise bark
of an oak tree.
A knowing smile
My eyes closed gently,
And my hands folded, still.
In a leopard casket.
With gold trim
and pink pillows
Is all I will leave behind.
That, And Vibrant memories
of a colorful woman
who spoke of love often
and never stopped creating.
A woman who gave her limbs
wholeheartedly to everything
she ever loved;
Equally.
accidents and
accomplishments.
pain and progress.
A brave woman
with feathers in her hair

And the moon clenched tightly
in the back of her jaw.

A woman who learned to tame fear.
Who in the end,
learned to treat it
as nothing more than a dare.

A divine challenge
A test to see if she
was worthy of heaven.
And she was.
She always was.

When I die I will not be alone.
I will take with me
my demons.
I will dance with them.
And when they start to grow too large
I will draw from my artillery:
my mother's courage,
my father's spirit,
and every single poem
I have birthed
in the name of love.
Even in death,
my art will keep me safe.
I will have learned to let it do this.
Those who loved me
will finally be free
those I loved
will forever be mine
And those who blamed me-
will finally know peace.

Womanhood: In this section, I challenge the traditional idea of what it means to be a woman. At the core of my being, I am a feminist. And I can only hope that you are too. Start a poem with the line "Women are..." and explain what and who they are to you, who they have been in your own life and in general. Take this time to reflect on all the women in your life and how multi-dimensional they are.

Gratitude

Pamela Antonacci, my Mommy. From the day I was born you have watched over me and always made sure I was given the space to create. to be myself. to be your daughter. You were my very first teacher, and if I survive this journey-- it will only be because you showed me how. I love you mommy.

Daddy. On days when I almost live up to who you thought I was; I know your absence is going to be felt even harder: college graduation, my child's first birthday, the release of this book-- these moments are incomplete without you. Thank you for my spirit.

Antoinette "Toni" Espino, my Sister Moon. You are the one person who has unfailingly loved and supported everything I do. You are the first to come to my rescue when shit gets real. You are the most loyal person I have ever known and the best sistermom I could ask for.

Natalie Patterson. It was you who taught me how to teach and write with honesty. Thank you for always being a mirror: for always telling me the truth, and for showing me how to wear my goddess with grace and integrity.

Venessa Marco. Thank you for being there even without being here. For supporting, loving and encouraging not only this book, but me. Always.

Yesika Salgado. Your never-ending love and support has helped grow me in so many ways. We are of the same heart. Thank you for always showing up when I need you the most.

114

Joel Jaimes. Plain and simple, this book literally wouldn't exist without you. You helped get it out of my head and into my hands. Thank you.

Yuriko Ruizesparza. Thank you for making me always feel like I am capable, reminding me of how far I've come, and inspiring me to be the woman I was meant to be.

Jimmy Valdez. If it weren't for you, I would have given up so many times. Not only on this project, but in general. Thank you for seeing the potential in me.

Da Poetry Lounge. Shihan, Dante, Poetri & Gimel: & Natalie Thank you for creating the space that raised me. DPL squad: Danielle, Fish, Jason, Edwin, Vanessa, Bird, Carolyn, Jasmine. Thank you for hugging me. and making me laugh. and molding me with your poems. Thank you for growing with me and for being my friends.

Hiram Sims & The CLI Mafia Without you, none of this would be possible. Hiram, you are the facilitator of our dreams. Thank you for believing in me.

&last but not least, THANK YOU to anyone who has ever supported me as an artist by buying my book. It means the world to me. You are helping me live my dream.

About the author

Angela Aguirre is a Chicana feminist poet and teaching artist based in Los Angeles who enjoys utilizing her creativity in meaningful ways. She writes about love, loss, identity, womanhood, heartbreak, and growth. She has been performing for the last 5 years, and has been a guest at a number of large events; such as the Adelante Mujer Latina conference and the Women for Racial Justice Breakfast. As a teaching artist, she has taught poetry at dozens of high schools, universities, and organizations such as InsideOut Writers, Homeboy Industries, the YWCA, and La Pintoresca Teen Education Center. Angela has a Bachelor's degree from California State University, Los Angeles in Communication Studies with an emphasis in Rhetoric and Social Change. In 2015 she completed the Community Literature Initiative Poetry program held at USC, and finished her book, *Confessions of a Firework*, which was published by the World Stage Press in 2016. As an artist and teacher, she hopes to inspire young people, particularly young women, to recognize their power and to work toward creating a better world through art. She is also one half of the Latina feminist collective Chingona Fire and is curating poetry events and platforms for women of color in Southern California.

My dad used to speak at NA meetings and conferences, and I want to leave you with one of his favorite ways to end his speeches:

"The next time someone sarcastically asks you if you think you're God's gift to this world… you tell them *I* said **you are**."

For videos and other information visit
Angelanicoleaguirre.com

To book performances or writing workshops email
angelanicoleaguirre@gmail.com

Follow me on Instagram
@Angelaloves

Friend me on Facebook
Angela Aguirre

Stay updated with Chingona Fire events on
Facebook and Instagram
@ChingonaFire

71004569R10073

Made in the USA
San Bernardino, CA
10 March 2018